Edible Schoolyard

A UNIVERSAL IDEA

Alice Waters

with Daniel Duane
Photographs by David Liittschwager

CHRONICLE BOOKS
SAN FRANCISCO

Text copyright © 2008 by Alice Waters.
Photographs copyright © 2008 by David Liittschwager,
unless otherwise noted.
Cover photograph copyright © 2008 by Suzie Rashkis.
Photographs provided courtesy of the Library of
Congress include page 4 by Edward Meyer and page 8,
photographer unknown.
Photograph page 18 copyright © 2008 by Beebo Turman.
Photographs, center, page 21;
page 65, top, copyright © 2008 by Ene Constable.
Photographer unknown, page 21, top and bottom;
page 74, second from bottom.

Library of Congress
Cataloging-in-Publication Data available.
ISBN: 978-0-8118-6280-6

Manufactured in China
This book is printed on 100% recycled paper.

Designed by Malgosia Szemberg
Typesetting by Patricia Curtan

10 9 8 7 6 5 4 3 2 1

Chronicle Books LLC
680 Second Street
San Francisco, California, 94107

www.chroniclebooks.com

For Tony Recasner and the Edible Schoolyard at the
Samuel J. Green Charter School, in New Orleans, Louisiana.
You have already proven that what began at the
Martin Luther King Jr. Middle School, in Berkeley, California,
is truly a universal idea.

Children's school and victory gardens on First Avenue between Thirty-fifth and Thirty-sixth Streets, New York City.

Foreword

I have had exactly two professions in my life. I spent four years teaching school, in my early twenties, and I've spent all of the intervening thirty-seven years running the one restaurant I own, in Berkeley, California. I got into teaching after college, when I moved to England and trained in Montessori education. I was a fervent student, and I loved Montessori's ideas about nourishing the whole child and encouraging children to learn by doing things with their own bodies and hands, by touching and tasting and smelling in an ongoing education of the senses. Then I found a job at the Berkeley Montessori School, a quiet little place at the corner of Shattuck Avenue and Francisco Street. Berkeley was in a period of enormous social upheaval, so it was an exciting time; every parent and teacher seemed to feel that we could bring about a more just society by working together. And yet no sooner had I settled into the job than I took a trip to Paris and felt a very different thunderbolt strike my life. French food, and the way it anchored French family life to an agricultural community and even to the seasons, was a revelation to me. Cooking dinners back in Berkeley, I began teaching myself the basics of French cuisine and dreaming of a restaurant where all my friends could come for tasty food and talk about politics—such as the right way to bring up our children and how to share this small planet. So I left teaching; I wasn't patient enough anyway. Then, with a few friends and partners, and the exuberant naiveté of youth, I opened a restaurant in an old house, a few blocks from the school. We called it Chez Panisse in honor of a beloved character from an old French movie, and we began sniffing around the back roads in search of delicious ingredients like the ones I'd tasted in France. The search wasn't easy, but we soon found ourselves on the doorsteps of organic farmers and ranchers and dairymen. Over the years, we built up a network of these suppliers, and that network came to define our food and our philosophy. That, in turn, led me back to education, and to the story I want to tell in this book—about a Berkeley middle school, and the creation of something called the Edible Schoolyard. It began as a way to bring that school into the local food network, so that nearby farmers might share their beautiful food with school children, and the school cafeteria, in turn, might help support local farmers. The Edible Schoolyard has been evolving for twelve long years now, and it has become the most important thing in my life. It has also served as the incubator for the universal idea that I term "Edible Education"—a hopeful and delicious way of revitalizing public education.

75
SCHOOL GARDENS

Report of the Fairview Garden School Association
Yonkers, N. Y.

BY

MRS. A. L. LIVERMORE
Chairman of the Executive Committee

Photo by Edward Mahoney
A Prize-winner

Published May, 1910

Growing the Garden . . .

Every day, when I drive between my restaurant and my home in Berkeley, I pass by a school. The sign on the wall says Martin Luther King Jr. Middle School, and I will never forget how neglected that place looked when I first took notice, fifteen years ago. The city of Berkeley has a great university, but its public schools rank among the poorest in the United States. They look much better now, after an earthquake retrofit project, but in the old days, that middle school was a run-down collection of sad old concrete buildings with peeling paint and a hard blacktop playground. Countless windows lay broken with no money to fix them, and a few lawns grew long and wild in the rainy season and then died and dried yellow in the summer. Graffiti was commonplace. The school looked so poorly tended, I wondered if it might not be abandoned. Then I learned that nearly 1,000 middle-school children were enrolled there, in grades six, seven, and eight. The school was also a center for teaching English as a Second Language, so it drew recent immigrants from all over the city, and more than twenty languages were spoken on campus, by children of every imaginable background. The state of the school made me wonder how those kids could possibly thrive in such an environment, and what message it sent about our culture's priorities. I began to think about my own teaching years and the faith I'd always had in public schooling, which I consider the last truly democratic institution in American life. Nearly every child goes to school, and it's the only place we can touch every one of them. For the first time in my adult life, during those daily commutes to and from work, I woke up to what was happening in public education, and I learned how badly things had fallen apart.

Working in the school garden was an integral part of the school day in the early 1900s.

I'm going to tell a positive story, here, shaped from my own memories of the next several years—about how a public school principal and a British gardener, a cook named Esther, and a lot of teachers, students, and parents made something beautiful happen in a blighted place. It became many things at once, the Edible Schoolyard, including a garden where children join their science teachers in growing and harvesting Brandywine tomatoes and golden raspberries along the way to learning about biology, ecology, and chemistry. Inside its working kitchen, a teacher might explain ancient history through the hand grinding of wheat berries into flour, and the baking of bread. And it has a communal dining table where many of our students eat the only shared meal of the day, and where the civilizing rituals of the table have become part of the larger curriculum. By the time a young girl has finished a delicious meal and returned her table scraps to the garden soil, and gone back to planting and harvesting with her science class, she is well on her way to understanding the cycle of life, from seed to table and back again—absorbing almost by osmosis the relationship between the health of our bodies, our communities, and the natural world.

Everyone involved has a story about the Edible Schoolyard, but my own begins with a journalist who visited my restaurant. He was a young, hard-working guy from a local newspaper, and somebody had told him about all our unusual suppliers and that I was thinking also about the use of land in cities, and about farming in empty lots. This sort of thing was new at the time, and surprising to people. Any empty lot, I'd realized, might be my next source of lettuce or fennel or tomatoes. Any overgrown backyard might produce the most beautiful blackberries I could ever hope to serve. While I told him about this, and about small farmers most people didn't know existed, I blurted out something incautious like, "You want to see a great example of how *not* to use land? You should come look at this enormous school in my neighborhood that looks like nobody cares about it. Everything wrong with our world is bound up in that place and in the way we treat children."

A few days after the article was published, I was in my office when a waitress appeared with an envelope someone had left at the front of the restaurant. The envelope had my name written on the front and a handwritten note from the principal of the middle school, Neil Smith. He'd read the article in the paper and wondered if I would look around the school with him, perhaps find a way to help. He mentioned that he agreed with much of what I'd said about land use, and that he'd planted a garden already in a courtyard not visible from the street. It's worth pointing out, here, that Neil was doing something very honorable. He was the school's fourth principal in two years, and he was so determined to make a difference that he wasn't content to read somebody's criticism in the paper; he felt that he had to contact me, and seek my help. I still remember walking down to meet Neil. He turned out to be a tall and slender man with a long neck and long fingers and very intense, penetrating brown eyes. He had the warmest, most intelligent smile and he quickly put me at ease. We went for a stroll around the schoolyard, over all that black asphalt rolling with the contours of the hill.

An entire wing of one building had been condemned, but there was no money for tearing it down and so it had simply been locked up. The cafeteria had been closed for years, because the school's population had doubled and the facility was too small. The only food the children could buy on campus came from a prefabricated building about the size of a shipping container. Parked in the middle of the asphalt, this building sold soda pop to the children during their recess and lunch hour, and it also sold something called a "walking taco," which is as perfect a symbol of a broken culture as I can imagine. Opening a plastic bag of mass-produced corn chips, the food workers would simply pour in a kind of beef-and-tomato slurry from a can. The kids would then walk away, eating on their own with no connection to one another. It seemed such a terrible waste—all that time and energy in a child's day, when hunger might be harnessed to open minds. Right then, I told Neil—who had the most striking intelligence and optimism about him—that *this* was where I could make a difference. I told him I'd love to start a garden on campus where students could grow and harvest whole-some food as part of their education. We could open a new kitchen, too, and teach students to cook the food they were growing, and even a cafeteria for sharing it with their classmates, and a way to recycle leftovers right back into soil.

You have to remember that nobody talked this way, in those days. So it wasn't a surprise when Neil laughed out loud. But I kept pushing, because Neil had called my bluff, inviting me down to his school. He'd said, in essence, "You want to tell reporters my school's a mess? Well, then how about helping me fix it?"

Now I was calling *his* bluff: "Okay, you really want my help? I think I know what I have to offer: Let's work together and change everything about the way children experience food at school."

"You're serious, aren't you?" Neil said.

I was.

He looked away and said something about the reactions he would get when he told exhausted, overworked public-school teachers they ought to spend time and energy on a revolutionary new farming-cooking-and-eating program that had nothing to do with the state's educational mandates. He said they would laugh him out of the room, and then have him committed.

"Well, it can't hurt to try," I said.

Neil said, "I think I'd better get back to you on this."

"Why? Why not just do it?"

"Let's just say I need to meet with my revolutionary committee."

A month went by, and then another month, but then Neil called at last. He'd brought up the idea with his parent-teacher association and a woman named Beebo Thurman had agreed to help. That was all Neil needed; one serious volunteer. He made clear that he was only ready for a garden; the kitchen and cafeteria would come later. I was delighted, but also panicked:

I knew this was going to take time and money, and I knew also that the school district had no surplus of either. So I asked all my dear friends for their help—in the form of money. Neil told me we'd do well to enlist the faculty, so I began inviting them for lunch at Chez Panisse, so they could experience the restaurant's food and understand where I was coming from. Entire faculty departments—all the science teachers, one day, humanities teachers, another—came to the restaurant, and I could feel that some of them were skeptical. The federal government demands a lot of teachers, insisting they teach every child a set number of lessons each term. But most of those teachers were lighter of spirit by the meal's end, and they certainly opened my eyes to something important: If this kitchen and garden had any chance of becoming real, there would have to be a way for teachers to teach. Math teachers, when they brought their children to this imaginary kitchen and garden, would have to see ways that baking could teach kids about fractions, history teachers that growing heirloom grains could teach children about the ancient world.

The schoolchildren and their parents were easier to convince. Half my restaurant's staff came to the gymnasium, one night, to throw a taco dinner fundraiser—which was mostly just a way to raise awareness, and ask the community for help. We built a wood fire outside, to simmer beans, and we set up long folding tables for making tortillas by hand. Wood smoke wafted around the room as the families filed inside—recent Thai immigrants and UC Berkeley professors, second-generation Indian families and African Americans whose grandparents had moved out west during the Second World War to work in the naval shipyards. Middle-school children aren't the most expressive—they're intensely concerned with fitting in and avoiding embarrassment. In fact, if you were planning an Edible Schoolyard from scratch, and you could pick any school at all, you'd be crazy to start with that age group. (It's a difficult time for most people, and one that very few remember fondly.) The need to be accepted and play it cool is so powerful as to be almost painful, and nobody wants to let on if they like something, for fear it'll be the wrong thing to like. But children that age also love doing things with their hands, and once they realized what we had in mind, they eagerly split into groups for patting masa. While the parents milled around and talked and ate chips and drank lemonade, and a few kids passed big bowls of guacamole, we set the first group of kids to work. Another hallmark of that age is a hunger for new skills, and the children were captivated by the feel of the dough and the pleasure of shaping it; they also adored the opportunity to stand around with their peers, chatting and joking and laughing. In fact, the first group had so much fun they refused to budge when their turn was up. Soon the second group had to join in and the third group, too, until we had more than a hundred middle-school kids from every imaginable background making tortillas together. We also had a whole bunch of adults, ourselves included, who thought we might just be onto something.

A month later, on a cold, clear day in February, I returned to the school with the restaurant staff and set up tables outside, at the end of the school day. We wanted to do something so magical and surprising and captivating that it would get everyone's attention, so a few of us ran over to the nearby Berkeley Horticultural Nursery and borrowed citrus trees. We used the trees to shape a glittering green oasis around the tables and then we draped white tablecloths and put out three sorbets that we had made from scratch: blood orange, tangerine, and Meyer lemon. When the final bell rang, the kids came running out of those big concrete buildings to head off to their various homes. Then they saw that curious scene, a grove of potted citrus trees, shining in the sun and surrounding a table with tubs of what looked like ice cream. They stopped in droves around the free sorbet. To get a scoop, the kids first had to sample each kind without being told which was which; then they had to guess at the flavor of each before saying which they liked the most. It goes against a kid's every instinct to eat something he or she can't identify, but by the time the sorbet was all gone, the guessing game had become the whole point, and we'd had five hundred students letting those flavors explode in their mouths.

We held a lot of meetings with landscape architects and gardeners, farmers and teachers and designers. We did our best to imagine how the garden should look, and we settled on the right site, an abandoned acre at the far uphill edge of the school. Neighboring homes abutted the lot, and a tangle of old trees and shrubs created a wilderness at one end. The other end of the site had several old portable classrooms left behind from the 1950s, and asphalt paths connecting them. We hauled away all but one of the buildings, and we had bulldozers tear up the asphalt. We tested the soil for pollutants—you never know what you'll find in an urban empty lot—and then a teacher named Beth Sonnenburg had her entire class stand shoulder to shoulder and walk the lot. Picking up rocks, they tossed them all aside, preparing the soil. Later, that very same class walked the lot again, this time scattering seed for a cover crop—bell beans and crimson clover, fenugreek, oats, and vetch to begin fertilizing the soil.

As that first year let out, and summer passed and the students came back in the fall, we found enough money that Terra Firma Farms, not far from Berkeley, could deliver a weekly box of produce for new after-school cooking classes, and for every sixth-grade classroom. Phoebe Tanner, another teacher who helped enormously in those early days, got to work developing lesson plans that used red peppers, broccoli, or whatever she got as teaching tools—holding up lettuce, one day, for example, and talking about photosynthesis. Phoebe sliced that lettuce right in front of the kids, and washed it afterward. She sliced orange carrots and deep-red tomatoes and made a dressing, and showed the class how eating a salad was our way of taking energy from plants that, in turn, have taken energy from the sun. The best part of all was a student who stood up at the end of class and began to clap—a charismatic girl who drove the whole mood of the classroom. Once the other kids realized what she was doing, they joined her in giving Phoebe a standing ovation.

An entrance to one of the main school buildings; a sign on the playground gate tagged with graffiti; and the view from the garden that looks out over the vast paved playground area behind the school buildings.

Cultivating discs are stranded in the hardpan of the newly cut ground; early plantings on the way to establishing a lush garden classroom; the quiet calm of the ramada welcomes students before class begins.

The faculty showed terrific openness, too, as we arranged for them to visit local organic farms and nearby gardens. We started vermiculture and a campus-wide recycling project that year, and built a wood-burning adobe oven. In our second spring, when the heavy winter rains had left our soil lush and saturated and when the warm sun brought out the first green cover crop, we got a windfall of new support. It came from Zenobia Barlow, director of the Center for Ecoliteracy, a local nonprofit devoted to precisely the kind of curriculum we hoped to create. With Zenobia's enthusiastic help and the Center's funding, we hired our first full-time garden director, David Hawkins, a thoughtful Englishman with dark brown eyes and brown hair over a weathered face.

David grew up in the rough public schools of England and he'd been so unhappy within the four walls of a classroom that he'd been expelled at least once. He'd found purpose in his early adulthood by working with kids involved in National Front racist organizations, young people who simply could not conform to the structured life of a classroom. He'd found ways to reach these children by spending time with them on so-called "adventure playgrounds" and also in arts centers and even on the streets, serving as a cross between an informal social worker and a teacher. David had a strong artistic streak, too, an understanding of how aesthetic beauty can be a kind of medicine. He had even apprenticed on an organic farm in Occidental, California. So by the time David started working with us, in that second spring, he was perfect for the job, and the job was just right for that moment in his life.

Summer vacation wasn't far off, so David asked Neil for a group of kids to put in a summer program—tough kids, preferably, from underprivileged backgrounds, the kind of kids who would benefit most from a healthy summer outdoors. David wanted to break ground right away, and begin building the hardscape of the garden, and he felt strongly that students should be involved from the start, laying out every footpath and flower bed. Left to myself, I would've tried to raise more money and hire landscape architects

to create a place that resonated with my own sense of beauty. And I would have done it in a week, or a month. But David had the beautiful insight that children should participate from the very start, so the garden wouldn't feel plopped down by self-impressed adults. He believed that something invaluable would emerge if we just gave our kids pick-axes and hoes and shovels, taught them how to work like professionals, and let them loose on an unformed place. Only in this way, David realized, would children become so proud of what they had accomplished as to feel forever connected to this new garden. He also sensed that if the very first group became attached to the garden, their attachment might infect the other children in the fall, who might wonder about this little miracle brought into being by their classmates. Perhaps later generations of schoolchildren would feel in their bones that this garden had been built by children like themselves, even if nobody ever told them so. They would just know by living—among the shapes and places those long-ago children created. They would intuit something of themselves in the very soil, and it would draw them in.

Neil rounded up a little group and I decided to bring lunch on the first day. After all, these were my first students! I thought to myself, *Okay, these kids are urban adolescents, so I'm going to bring food they already know and like, and not a single thing that's unfamiliar.* I had a favorite peach farmer deliver an extra box to the restaurant, because everybody loves peaches and, to my mind, these were the most glorious peaches on earth, the kind that can change your life with a bite. Then I drove to the industrial part of town to get tacos at a Mexican restaurant owned by my brother-in-law. I was in a hurry, speeding around, and when I got back to the school I piled all the tacos on the peach box and walked over to the empty lot. Hot sun was just burning away the fog and I was excited to see what the kids had done, and to share food with them. But then I discovered that we don't all picture the same thing when we think of tacos. Some of us see soft tortillas with *carne asada* and salsa verde, but some of us see factory-folded crispy taco shells and hamburger meat in red sauce, and if we don't see what we're used to seeing, we don't see tacos and we don't eat. As for the peaches, I'd forgotten about the problem of peach fuzz, and how it can frighten a kid who isn't used to it, regardless of how glorious the fruit might be. I went home that day with a lot of uneaten food and a broadened perspective. But over time, working with David, the children made so many things with their own hands that we brought taco fixings again—with all the ingredients kept apart, this time, so the children could assemble their own. That's when we learned an enduring lesson: No matter how picky kids are, they are infinitely more likely to eat food they've made with their own hands.

Soon it was time to plant our very first food crops, so David put his rough-and-tumble crew into a van and drove them to a forest. The idea was to harvest willow branches, bring them back to our still-empty lot, and build traditional mud-and-wattle planting beds. The van broke down en route, and they lost a lot of time in a bleak yard that repaired school buses, but they finally got to the willow thicket and David led the kids down a trail toward a creek. A breeze picked up, bringing the smell of the San Francisco Bay, and David handed out garden shears—*loppers,* he called them, in his English manner. He showed the kids how to cut the branches, tie them into bushels, and haul them back to the van. These city kids didn't consider this to be any fun at all. One boy even wondered aloud if David shouldn't be paying them. In a flash, David realized what was wrong: The lives these children led had almost no room for that greatest of childhood necessities, free play. So he stopped everyone, sat them all down on the ground, and gave them an impromptu lesson in the construction of a bow and arrow. Running around in the woods for a while, their spirits came back to life. Then they gladly piled the remaining branches in the back of the van and climbed in front with their muddy shoes and their hands streaked green from the willow bark. Back at the garden, David taught the basics of mud-and-wattle construction, helping the kids to weave little walls that would hold the soil up high. All that day, and the next and the next, they worked and worked until they had three raised beds completed and ready to fill with soil.

Just in time, our city government offered free compost: Twenty-four tons arrived in a gigantic, specialized dump truck, creating a vast and smelly pile eight feet high and many times that wide. David asked for a show of hands from kids willing to shovel it into wheelbarrows, and another show of hands from those willing to shuttle the wheelbarrows back and forth to the mud-and-wattle beds. When he'd taught the first group how to bring a shovel up against the base of the compost pile and let the compost tumble in, he walked off to show the others how to fill a bed. When he returned to the main pile, he found all of the wheelbarrows pushed near the apex and the kids filling them by digging a giant volcanic crater. It wasn't the most efficient way of working, and it certainly wasn't the way David had told them to get the job done, but he quickly recognized that this was the way the children had found joy in their work, so he encouraged them. Caves appeared next, tunneled from the crater out toward the volcano-like slopes, and then the boys and girls were all looking through at each other and laughing in the sunshine. That moment, as much as any, marks for me the true beginning of the Edible Schoolyard—the instant at which our dream came to life.

Mâche and arugula, mustard greens and kale, bok choi, carrots and turnips and garlic and potatoes—these were among the very first foods David and his kids planted. Once the seeds had gone into those first mud-and-wattle beds, and as more and more beds took shape and began to fill with soil and sprout new crops, Neil promised we could at last start a kitchen. It was the fall term of our third year, and he gave us the okay to reopen the disused kitchen. If you like ancient ruins, or the mystery of long-abandoned places, you would've enjoyed waking up that old room with me. Martin Luther King Jr. Middle School had been built in 1921, and the cafeteria and

kitchen, despite their disrepair, were a testament to how much more money schools had in those days. The school district couldn't spare a single dollar for returning them to their former glory—the money wasn't there—but the superintendent of schools made sure nobody stood in our way, and he offered his own weekend time to help out. So we got to work at clearing away garbage and cobwebs, and then we hired our first kitchen director, a chef named Esther Cook, who'd grown up on a farm.

Esther has since told me that in opening those old doors, and wandering those rooms by herself, she knew she had opened the door to a new chapter in her life. There were a few strange and forbidding elements, like the dumbwaiter in one wall, going down to where? A nearby door creaked open and Esther saw stairs, so she turned on a flashlight and walked slowly and carefully into a kind of crypt—a series of dusty, silent underground rooms. One of the rooms was filled from floor to ceiling with old, broken chairs, and the glass from the few windows, all of which were up high, at the level of the outside ground, lay shattered. She found another room that had once been a kind of teacher's lunchroom, a place they could smoke cigarettes and call up to the kitchen for food, and where asbestos insulation now hung frayed off pipes in the ceiling. And, lastly, there were two old bathrooms—the only two bathrooms available. After a quick look inside them, Esther ran back up to the kitchen, which was a joy by comparison.

Not a week later, when the spring term began and Esther's first group of kids was about to come see her, she walked up to the garden to ask David what she could cook. The only thing ready that day, as it happened, was kale; all the other crops had either been used up by evening cooking classes or were still immature.

Esther felt a kind of dread sweep through her. "Kale, huh? That's all?"

David nodded. That was all he had.

Kale, Esther assumed, was the last thing any middle-school child would eat, and she loathed the thought of beginning this unlikely journey with such a doomed food. But she did her best, showing kids all the different ways you can slice bread, and how to sauté the greens in olive oil and garlic. Then the kids toasted the bread slices and began piling kale on top of them. They took a long time with this, making careful little patterns, and then they placed them all on a platter and brought the platter to a table for the other kids to share. Esther was so nervous, that day, watching the first kid stare at the platter. After a long time, this girl finally took a piece of toast with greens and passed the platter. The next kid, a boy whose parents lived across town, did the same thing: He stared and stared before suddenly making his selection. When the third kid also did the same, Esther realized what was happening: They wanted to eat the ones they personally had made! And once they found a toast they'd put together with their own hands, the kale vanished in no time. All of us realized just how surprising a child's taste can be, and were reminded how much more likely they are to enjoy something they've created with their own hands. Esther went home giddy that day because she knew that if kids could love kale they could love anything— *Wait until we have strawberries!* she thought. *Or late-summer tomatoes!*

Over time, our understanding of middle-school kids began to deepen. We realized that many of them felt things they never showed on the surface. One girl's mother told Phoebe that this girl had a pair of special shoes just for gardening, and that she loved her garden days so much she always set out those shoes the night before, to remember them. Phoebe had to hide her astonishment, because that girl never let on at school that she liked the garden one bit. David had a boy who would simply sit and watch the other kids, and never help out. No matter how hard David tried, the boy refused to participate. But at the end of the session, at a little gathering for parents, the boy's mother walked up and said, "David, thank you so much for being so nice to my son. The garden has completely changed him!" David was polite, but in truth he had no idea what she was talking about. "How do you mean?" he asked. "Well, my son used to come home and play video games and watch TV all night," said the boy's mother. "Now he comes home and talks and talks about the garden and everything happening there. He talks to the family and our friends and neighbors, and now he has started making up stories about gardens and plants."

Another time, David gave two girls a box containing parts for a new wheelbarrow. He just handed them a wrench and a screwdriver and left them alone to assemble the thing. The girls did a fine job and David didn't think much of it, but at the end of the term, the two girls told him it was a highlight of their year. They said that nobody had ever trusted them to do something like that.

Then came the wonderful day that Esther let students make pancakes from scratch. As each class came into the kitchen, they found nothing on the tables except the recipe, written out. Dividing into groups, they had to do everything: find the ingredients, measure the right amounts, mix the batter, turn on the stove. One of the teachers found this frightening and said to Esther, "I am so worried they won't be able to do this. It'll make them feel badly about themselves." Esther tried to reassure her, but the teacher kept saying, "Esther, I want you to realize, this could be a disaster for my kids." And it's true: There were runny pancakes, and pancakes that would've made great Frisbees, and others that could've been hockey pucks, and others that were delicious, but they were all still pancakes, and you would've thought those kids had climbed Mount Everest, they were so proud. Best of all, that teacher had to leave the room to wipe tears from her eyes.

We did have awkward moments—mishaps and slip-ups and things that never went as planned. Kids had to walk clear across campus just to bring the kitchen compost to the garden—hoisting big buckets, and trying not to spill. There were neighbors who complained about smoke from our pizza oven, and teachers who became frustrated. A homeless man lived in the greenhouse for a while, and somebody seems to have harvested a lot of food occasionally to take home. But the garden continued to thrive and draw in new believers, and Esther somehow made her kitchen a part of the life of the school, in just the way a home kitchen can anchor the life of a family. I saw this with my own eyes, dropping by and watching how much the kids admired Esther, but also in the stories Esther told, like about a group of siblings she met. The first one to show up in her kitchen was a boy who was plainly hungry—truly hungry, as in badly needing food. So when class was over, she asked him very quietly what he'd had for breakfast that day. He hadn't eaten breakfast; he never ate breakfast. Esther taught him right then and there to take eggs from the refrigerator and cook them for himself. She told him to do this every single day before school, without ever asking. Just come and do it. As the year went on, Esther grew close to that boy and his siblings and they all came to see the kitchen as a special place to come for advice and conversation. The role of a teacher and mentor in a young student's life can be complex, but the influence of such a teacher at a critical time can have life-changing effects. Esther's young friend stayed in touch and years later was proud to tell her that he was in college studying the culinary arts. He and Esther now meet at the farmers' market to taste and brainstorm how to prepare the season's offerings.

As for the rest of us, the teachers and parents and volunteers, there's just something infectious about the idea of an Edible Schoolyard—it's such a hopeful and uplifting notion that it just takes hold of people in the same way it took hold of me. It makes people want to help out, as a way of believing in a world where such a thing could really happen. I saw this spell fall over more and more teachers, as time went by, and also over volunteers who wandered in from their various lives, offering to help—like the man with a portable lumber mill who turned a fallen acacia tree into rough lumber. That was in our fourth year, just before ten young women from the University of Montana drove across the American west to learn basic carpentry and help our students turn the rough lumber into an elegant shade structure.

A wood artist showed us how to weave exquisite fences from tree limbs, and another helped the kids build a strong and simple toolshed from redwood. All of these artisans passed on wisdom to the garden workers and the kids themselves, and every time I dropped by, I was struck by the children's craftsmanship. Like budding professionals, our kids laid out beautiful new footpaths and mended fences. More and more crops were going in—citrus and apple trees, plums and ground cherries and hazelnuts, figs, kiwis and even edible bamboo—and the students built very professional crop terraces from broken chunks of recycled concrete. David had a nose for materials and techniques that didn't require the use of dangerous power tools, and a strong faith in the ability of young people to do real work. He also had a great sense of play, encouraging them to build whimsical things such as a giant birds' nest, shaped from tree branches and twigs and keyed to a study of bird behavior. The nest was held together with mud and big enough to hold four kids sitting all at once, which of course they loved.

By our sixth year, the children were picking blackberries from their own bushes and mulberries from their own tree, and learning the joy of a summer tomato eaten right off their own vines. We'd even begun a tradition with incoming sixth graders, allowing them to pick corn right off the stalk, shuck it with their own hands, grill it over a wood fire, and eat it right there in the garden. Year seven saw the start of an herb garden, with plants for making tea and flavoring foods, and a big *Dia de los Muertos* celebration with an altar in the garden and Pan de los Muertos baked in our kitchen. We had a big holiday wreath sale that year, too, as a fundraiser before the Christmas vacation—giving away pounds of produce in the process. And when it was time for the statewide testing called SAT9, we offered a free, healthy breakfast to 400 students on each of two days.

David did eventually move on to other projects—I remain forever grateful to him. Likewise to Neil Smith, who took on a vital role at the headquarters of the school district, designing curricula for the entire city. But Phoebe and Beth and other teachers kept bringing their classes to the

garden, and an English teacher named Josie Gerst made it possible for us to host school celebrations such as Family Writing Night and the English Learners Dinner. And Esther grew ever more devoted to her kitchen as the years went by, and she became ever more beloved by the students of Martin Luther King Jr. Middle School. I'll never forget hearing about a group of her students who had graduated and gone on to Berkeley High School; as ninth grade began, they learned that a tragedy had befallen a boy they'd known at King. The place they came to mourn was Esther's kitchen, a half-dozen kids showing up out of the blue and asking Esther if they could make tea the way she had always shown them. Gathering the herbs from the garden, boiling the water, letting it steep—the kids spent the whole afternoon with Esther. She has since told me that in addition to the great gift of being brought into their lives in that way, the kids also reaffirmed for her one of our fundamental convictions, one of the very beliefs that made us want this project to work in the beginning: the belief in the power of the table to bring people together and give them a place to commune. One of the boys played a guitar while the rest remembered their classmate and cried and talked about the boy's family and how they must be suffering. Esther encouraged them to pick a bouquet from the garden and carry it to that boy's parents.

In our eighth year, we cooked yet another big free breakfast for state-wide testing—vegetable soup, macaroni and cheese, and oatmeal. We lost our kitchen that year—the city shut it down while they reinforced the old building against earthquakes. But we salvaged everything we could, from shelves and tables down to old scraps of lumber, and we carried it all up to the one bungalow left among the planting beds in the garden. A group of teachers gave their time, parents volunteered, and together we created a light-filled temple for the honest work and simple joy of preparing food. Determined to make the place utterly unlike an institutional kitchen, we had a local artisan fashion magnificent tabletops from poured concrete, and we mounted them on heavy timbers. Another local craftsman painted the walls in soft, soothing colors, and we built open storage spaces for every kitchen

Scarab Beetle

Wolf Spider

Termites

Geophilid Centipede

Flat-backed Millipede

Funnel weaving Spider

Lady Bug

Roly Po[

Beetle Larva

Lithobiid Centipede

Carabid Beetle

tool, so the eye could wander from a worn stone mortar and pestle, to a hand-press for making tortillas, to an apple press. Old French illustrations, framed and hung between the big, sun-flooded windows, showed ancient heirloom fruits and vegetables; and Esther hung colorful prayer flags over the dishwashing area and let the teachers inscribe them with encouraging thoughts for the students. Most of all, we used this place to express a core belief: Beauty is not a luxury; it is a means of lifting the human spirit and of giving richness to everyday life.

Fifteen years after Neil Smith called my bluff, and twelve years after David Hawkins broke ground with his summer recruits, three hundred public schoolchildren from the sixth grade through the eighth visit the Edible Schoolyard every week. They make a first trip with a science teacher, walking alone through the garden and responding to prompts like "pick a yellow cherry tomato and eat it," or "smell the rose geranium." Then comes a second visit, also with that science teacher, to pick and grill and eat those first ears of corn, savoring the miracle of just-picked grain in a way that almost nobody does anymore. After that, the children settle into a varied rhythm of visits that runs for all three years they spend at the school, always in ninety-minute science sessions shaped around plant structure or decomposition or something similar, and always beginning with an outdoor meeting on a pile of hay bales—except when it rains.

There's always an opening talk about the four or five garden jobs that need doing, which nearly always means mulching and weeding, planting and composting—the fundamental work of growing food. The teacher and gardener suggest something the kids might talk about while they work, such as which plants are dormant plants or a meal they might make with one of the crops. Then students form their own groups and head off with an adult to gather tools, pull on rubber boots, pick up baskets and go harvest something—mulberries, or pears, or zucchini. And they get to pick a place in the garden to call their own, a place to sit alone to do their required journal writing—a practice that shows us, again and again, and in their own beautiful voices, how porous children are to the natural world. "The bees, the spiders, the ants," wrote one sixth-grader, "the rolly-pollies, the bugs, the sound, the sky, the birds, the clouds, the yellow leaves . . . the leaves rustle with hidden secrets that even the laziest man would be dying to know. And the bees, gracefully floating from flower to flower, sing of flowers and gnomes and fairies who never seem to show themselves to anything but the bees, the birds, and the trees. I smell fresh air . . . I see beautiful white flowers . . . and figs. I wonder, when are figs ready to eat?"

The humanities teachers have grown to love using the kitchen to enrich their classes, and they've become expert at making connections between food and scholarship. While teaching about Neolithic times, for example, they'll take the kids over to the kitchen, have them tie on aprons, wash their hands, and join Esther in hand-grinding grain berries in a stone mortar and then making bread to eat warm, right from the oven. Or while learning about the social hierarchy of Medieval Europe, the kids will divide into groups representing Lords and serfs; while the Lords got the very best fruits and vegetables from the garden, and perhaps some meat, the serfs only received roots and grains. Everyone learns about the crucial nutrients missing from the serfs' diet, and how serfs didn't have a lot of teeth, and how they made soft meals like porridge or soup. The kids from the Lord's table get to walk over and claim ten percent of the serfs' food—quite a lesson in social justice!

But so much beautiful produce is coming out of the garden, these days, that everyone gets to make food they love, such as artichoke fritters and a soup of pumpkin and kale. We've also hired a devoted program director, Marsha Guerrero, who, among other things, had the beautiful idea of starting a chicken coop. Our small flock of Araucana and Rhode Island Red chickens now roam free during the day, eating snails and mulching with their feet, and we lock them in the coop at night, so they won't wander off or get taken by animals. We've also added a double-burner propane range to the garden, so that kids can fry those utterly fresh eggs right there, and grasp that immediate connection between the plants, the snails, the chickens, and their own sustenance. They can still pick fresh lemon verbena leaves, right from the ground, and drop them into boiling water to make a soothing herbal tea. Every class session concludes with the meal at the big table, where the children improvise a centerpiece from sweet pea flowers or fresh lemons or just a big old wooden spoon—and learn basic etiquette, such as not eating until everyone has been served, or asking politely for food to be passed. Children of that age often hesitate before talking in a big group, so Esther has developed a set of talking cards—index cards with good questions for starting a discussion. She now hands them out before the meal, so that even the basic skills of civilized communication become a part of the journey.

The idea of the Edible Schoolyard has grown beyond our one acre. The Samuel. J. Green Charter School, in New Orleans, Louisiana, now has an Edible Schoolyard of its own. Growing and cooking their very different food, in their very different climate and culture, they've taught us that no two Edible Schoolyards can be alike. They've also helped articulate our core mission: to awaken every American child's senses toward a new relationship with food, one in which deliciousness comes first and good health and well being are the happy result.

The original Edible Schoolyard has also grown: A local farmer named Bob Cannard gave us a dozen young olive trees to plant around the perimeter; they've taken root and we've begun to cure our own olives. The shade structure and tool shed still stand, along with a nursery for seedling starts and a complex composting structure. The flower beds are quite distinct from the herb beds, and last year alone, our single acre of soil produced 300 ears of corn, 289 eggs, and 1059 pounds of vegetables, including carrots and chard, beets and broccoli, bok choi, tatsoi, potatoes, onions, green beans, spinach, cucumbers, basil, thyme, scallions, lemons, radishes, fennel, cilantro, cabbage, and *twelve varieties* of apples. I'm leaving a lot out, and the neighborhood deer know it—they can do a lot of damage overnight, far more than the teenagers who sneak in to party on weekends.

But the most important visitors are the thousand scheduled guests we get every year, including American educators and politicians, foreign guests from Kenya and Ghana, once even Charles, the Prince of Wales, hoping the Old World might again learn from the New.

When these people walk into the Edible Schoolyard for the first time, and see American children eating a civilized and delicious meal around a shared table, and talking to one another—as humans have done for millennia—they know in their hearts that Edible Education is just plain right. Ten years ago, our culture might not have been ready, but no longer will anyone tell you

there's something elitist about awakening a child's senses to healthful, delicious food grown by local farmers or by the kids themselves. No longer can anyone say that only the privileged should worry about learning to cook good simple meals in their own kitchens, and share them with family and friends. These are the bedrock pleasures and values on which our agrarian democracy was founded, and they remain the key link between our private selves, the health of our bodies and our planet, and each American's power to influence positive change.

Our lives have become much too fast, too separated from the values our farming forebears knew without knowing. Runaway obesity and diabetes are the consequences, along with the disintegration of the American family and the harm we've done to the natural environment. The transformation of school lunch, around the idea of Edible Education, is a rare opportunity to reverse all that. It will take money from our state and federal governments, and advocacy by our leaders, to change course on a ship this big. It also won't be easy, because it can't happen just by lecturing kids on nutrition, or putting salad bars in cafeterias. Edible Education is an experience, a long-term proposition. It is an integration of a school garden and kitchen and cafeteria into the very core of the teaching mission, from kindergarten forward. It's a way of making sure that children grow up feeling the soil with their own fingers, harvesting its bounty in the American sunshine, and watching their own hands make the kind of beautiful, inexpensive food that can nourish the body and the spirit. Only then will the next generations of Americans know that we don't just vote in the ballot box, we vote for the kind of world we want every time we choose what to eat. Only then will our children feel for themselves why saving open space for farming isn't just a nice idea, and why the upside of a global economy doesn't extend to food—which should travel the shortest distance possible before being sold, in the interest of human health and happiness, of our local economies, and of our natural environment.

But the time is right. There is a fast-spreading awareness that progressive change must come in this country, and that anything might once again be possible. In a nation where far too many people harm their health and the environment by eating poorly, public school lunch presents an enormous opportunity: Right there, in the middle of every child's school day, driven by his own hunger and his own taste, lies all this time and energy set aside and devoted to food. When people realize that we have the power to turn school lunch into something far more than an unhealthy afterthought, or a way of filling ourselves at the lowest price, with no thought to consequences, it's difficult to argue against spending the money, no matter what it might cost. As for any worry that Edible Education can't work, we know from our experiment at Martin Luther King Jr. Middle School that when children are encouraged to grow and cook and enjoy wholesome, delicious food all together, from the seed to the table and back again, in an atmosphere of caring and beauty, they fall in love with its lessons.

All you have to do to be convinced is come see for yourself—come watch children from all walks of life making salads with ten different kinds of lettuce, or patting together Indian samosas from potatoes and onions and garlic they've dug with their own fingers. All it takes is the kind of walk I make a few times a year, from my restaurant down to the Edible Schoolyard for yet another look at kids covered in red raspberry juice, foraging among the vines, or elbow-deep in the dirt, planting amaranth seedlings, or laughing and talking around a kitchen table while they shell peas for their friends. And although I drift away to other projects during most summers when the school quiets down, I always feel those memories welling up again in late August, when it's garden season again. And that's when I take that first walk of the year, out my restaurant's side door and onto busy Shattuck Avenue—the same Shattuck Avenue on which I once worked at the Berkeley Montessori School. It's a warm day, more often than not, and the quiet, leafy streets let my mind wander untroubled to the place I'm headed—the place where late summer means sunflowers over my head, and shell beans filling out their string trellises, and hollyhocks and larkspur blooming all around. As I walk that last block, and my feet finally leave the pavement and step onto the same soft ground where bulldozers once scraped up black asphalt and where Beth's long-ago kids plucked up all the rocks, the ground where David's first summer gang spread out the city compost and where others planted trees, and where all those generations of students have since nourished themselves on food they've grown and harvested and cooked precisely to share with one another, I feel ever more convinced that Edible Education isn't just a lucky miracle at one public school; it is a truly universal idea.

Principles of Edible Education

Food is an Academic Subject

A school garden, kitchen, and cafeteria are integral to the core academic
mission of the school, so that ecology and gastronomy help bring alive
every subject, from reading and writing to science and art.

School Provides Lunch for Every Child

From preschool through high school, every child is served a wholesome,
delicious meal, every day. Good food is a right not a privilege.
Providing it every day brings children into a positive relationship
with their health, their community, and the environment.

Schools Support Farms

School cafeterias buy seasonally fresh food from local, sustainable
farms and ranches, not only for reasons of health
and education, but as a way of strengthening local food economies.

Children Learn by Doing

Hands-on education, in which the children themselves do the work
in the vegetable beds and on the cutting boards, awakens
their senses and opens their minds, both to their core academic
subjects and to the world around them.

Beauty is a Language

A beautifully prepared environment, where deliberate thought
has gone into everything from the garden paths to the plates on the tables,
communicates to children that we care about them.

Right there, in the middle of every devoted to the feeding of children. school lunch from an afterthought for our health, our environment, and

school day, lies time and energy already
We have the power to turn that daily
into a joyous education, a way of caring
our community.

German Dumplings

A food that I remember are German Dumplings. It was a night where me, my sister Ellen, and my brother Rob were cooking. We decided to make a new recipe for German Dumplings. It took a very long time to make them, but when we were done, they were delicous. They were made of some batter, chives, and bacon. This was all fried in butter. It had a buttery taste along with a small crunch from the bacon and chives. The batter had a lovely taste also. The butter was probably the part that stuck out most. It provided a wonderful after taste of fried butter. Some of the bacon taste leaked into the rest of the dumpling, sending a lovely flavor. The strong taste of the chives also provided a good taste. It was wonderful

RECYCLE
MIXED PAPERS

Students appreciate using real tools, such as 8-inch chef's knives, and there is no shortage of jobs for everyone in the kitchen. Classes begin with a discussion of ingredients and conclude with a shared meal. A student copies a recipe to prepare for her family at home.

Recipes & Lessons from the Edibl

The students cook in groups of ten. The recipes are designed to introduce them to a variety of foods, and to keep many hands busy, working side by side with the pleasant tasks of chopping, mincing, peeling, shelling, measuring, mixing, and of course, tasting. Here are a few sample recipes.

Soups

Autumn Harvest Soup
Won Ton Soup
Butternut Squash Soup
Black Bean Stew
Carrot and Tomato Soup
Garden Gazpacho
Kale and Potato Soup
Tortilla Soup
Spring Vegetable Soup

Eggs and Dairy

Coriander "Green" Eggs
Fresh Herb Butter
Rainbow Chard Frittata
Homemade Ricotta Cheese
Spanish Egg and Potato

Grains and Pasta

Chinese Noodle Salad
Egyptian Pasta with Lentils
Mexican Rice with Peas
Millet Crackers
Basil and Tomato Pizza
Potstickers
Soft Polenta with Cheese
Vegetable Fried Rice
Winter Greens and Bulgur
Apple and Carrot Salad

Salads

Bread Salad
Armenian Lentil Salad
Tomato Salad
Salad for Autumn
Thai Cabbage Salad

Sauces

Cilantro Coconut Chutney
Fresh Tomato Sauce
Garam Masala
Jicama and Mango Salsa
Herb Sauce
Sesame Soy Dressing
Shallot Vinaigrette
Three Citrus Dipping Sauce
Guacamole
Tomatillo Salsa
Garlic Mayonnaise

Vegetables

Curried Peas and Potatoes
Egg Rolls
Ethiopian Greens
Fried Green Okra
Fried Yams
Latkes with Apple Sauce
Pumpkin Curry
Roasted Plantains
Saag Paneer
Sautéed Kale and Beets
Kenyan Vegetable Stew
Zucchini Fritters

Cucumber-Lime Cooler serves 6–8

Pour 8 cups of water into a pitcher. Add ¾ cup sugar (or ½ cup honey) and stir until the sugar is dissolved. Juice 12 limes; to get the most juice from the limes, roll them back and forth on the table under your palm, until they are soft. Add the juice to the water and sugar. Wash, peel, and grate, using the medium holes of a box grater, 1 medium cucumber (you can leave the peel on if you are using an English cucumber). Add the grated cucumber to the pitcher and stir well. Try substituting watermelon for the cucumber.

Carrot-Raisin Salad serves 4–6

This salad of vegetables and fruit has universal appeal, especially to younger students.

Wash and peel 10 carrots. Grate the carrots into a bowl. Add 1 cup raisins and mix well. Eat the salad like this or serve it in a little lettuce leaf. If you want, you can make a little dressing by stirring 1 tablespoon lemon juice and some salt together. Whisk in 3 tablespoons olive oil and toss with the carrots and raisins.

Spring Vegetable Ragout serves 4–6

With this ragout, students taste foods at their peak ripeness and learn that not everything is available all the time. This simple recipe involves lots of shelling of peas and fava beans and creates the pleasant experience of sharing work and conversation.

Shell 3 pounds fava beans. Put the shelled beans into boiling water for 1 minute. Drain and rinse under cold water. Slip off the second skin. Shell 2 pounds peas. Wash, peel, and slice 6 baby carrots. Trim off the roots and outer layer from 3 spring onions, and chop. Chop 1 tablespoon each, mint, thyme, and parsley leaves. Measure 1 cup water. Heat 3 tablespoons

olive oil in a large, heavy skillet. Add the chopped onions, carrots, and fava beans and cook over medium heat for 5 minutes, stirring occasionally. Add the water, peas, and chopped herbs. Bring to a boil, then turn down to a simmer and cook for 3 minutes. Season to taste.

Bread Salad serves 4–6

We use day-old bread, which the students love to tear and toast. Preparing the herbs is an exciting way to discover the differences in their intense aromas and flavors.

Preheat the oven to 350°F. Tear ½ loaf unsliced rustic bread into crouton-sized pieces and bake on a sheet pan until crisp, but not browned, about 8 minutes. Meanwhile, wash, core, and dice 6 tomatoes. Wash, peel, and dice 4 cucumbers. Clean and dice 1 bell pepper. Chop ½ cup each parsley and mint leaves (or other herbs, such as chervil, basil, and thyme). Combine in a large bowl 3 tablespoons lemon juice, 1 teaspoon salt, ½ cup olive oil, ½ teaspoon pepper, and 1 clove garlic, peeled and crushed. Whisk together until salt is dissolved. Add all the chopped herbs and vegetables and gently mix. Add the toasted bread and mix well. Taste for seasoning and add more lemon juice, salt, pepper, or oil, as needed. Let sit 10 minutes before serving to allow the flavors to marry.

Red Bean Stew serves 4–6

The winter larder is filled with dried beans, coriander seeds saved from cilantro plants, and garlic. Students choose a variety of beans, for shape, color, and size. We like it with crusty bread and butter; sometimes the students make the butter by shaking cream in a jar, by hand.

Peel and chop 3 cloves garlic, 5 carrots, and 2 onions. Wash 2 bunches of greens (kale, chard, collards), drain, remove the stems, and chop the leaves roughly. Measure 2 cups cooked red beans (other beans may be substituted for the red beans), 2 cups tomato sauce, and 10 cups vegetable stock. Measure and combine ½ teaspoon each pepper flakes, coriander seeds, cumin seeds, and 1 bay leaf. When all the ingredients are ready, heat ¼ cup olive oil in a heavy-bottomed pot. Add the chopped garlic, carrots, onions, and spices. Cook over medium heat, stirring occasionally, for 5 minutes. Stir in the beans, tomato sauce, greens, vegetable stock, salt, and pepper. Bring to a boil then turn down to a simmer and cook until the greens are tender, about 10 minutes. Season to taste with salt.

Potato Smash with Kale serves 6–8

Mashing keeps many hands busy and the students like the taste and color of potato skins that are added to the "smash." It is delicious made with sweet potatoes.

Boil 4 pounds of potatoes (unpeeled), until tender. Drain. Wash 3 bunches of kale, drain, remove the stems, and chop the leaves roughly. Measure ¾ cup milk. Peel 7 cloves garlic and chop fine. Heat 3 tablespoons olive oil in a large heavy skillet, add the chopped garlic and cook for 30 seconds. Add the kale and cook, stirring occasionally, until tender, about 10 minutes. Add a little water if the pan gets dry and the greens start to stick. While they are still warm, smash the cooked potatoes in a ricer or with a potato masher. Put into a large bowl and add the milk and salt and pepper to taste. Mix well. Add the cooked kale and stir well to combine.

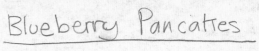

Blueberry Pancakes

Emma
1/25/02

One morning I woke up to the smell of worm blueberries. I looked in the kitchen and saw my dad at the stove, make blueberry pancakes. It smelled so delishous. I set the table and every one seemed to come to the table folowing the wonderful smell. We sat around the table ready. My dad put them on the table and we all dove in. Sometimes the blueberries were so sweet you don't have to use syrup. I will never forget that morning.

Assata

Memorble Cooking Moment

My most memorble cookig moment was when I was 8yrs old Me my mother and Father had just arrived in Africa at my Aunt Roses house and she had a whole feast for us. There was this jiggley food that looked like grits in the shape of a cake. It had chicken and suase all over it. My father said I had to eat 2 pieces of it. I tried to back out of it but he said I had to. Then I put the first bite of it in my mouth and it tatesed magical delouis. It was like magic in my mouth. I later learned that it was just Corn meal sired up with chicken and sauce It was great

Breads

Apple Lemon Muffins
Whole-Wheat Egg Bread
Currant Scones
Mildred's Cornbread
Empanadas
Sweet Potato Biscuits
Focaccia
French Toast
Popovers

food memories …

Drinks

Yogurt Berry Smoothie
Garden Herb Tea
Cucumber-Lime Cooler
Mint Lemonade
Carrot and Orange Juice

The fruit tree that I climbed on

Carrie
11/26/02

I remember when I was about 7 years old, I had an orange tree that I always climbed. It was a great tree to climb. The oranges were so good! They were so much better than in the grocery stores. It was a very hot day and me and my friends next door decided to grab some from the tree and make orange juice just by squeezing it into a cup. So we squeezed and squeezed! It was very sweet. Sometimes instead of squeezing the juice into the cup we squeezed it into our mouths. I remember perfectly the very sweet taste.

My First Tamale

12/3/04
Mr. Hopkin

The first time I had a tamale was when I was six years old. I remember seing my mom prepearing the dough. She had gave me a little piece to play with. It was really fun but it had gotten stuck on my both hands. My mom had made two different fillings. She had made one with meat and the other meat with chili. I had the one with just meat.

They were so good. The dough part was nice and soft. They were sort of hot but the sour cream cooled it down. I really enjoyed having that tamale it was the first and the best.

Sweets

Chocolate Chip Cookies
Raspberry Cream Puffs
Strawberry Crêpes
Lemon Poppy Seed Muffins
Lime and Pepita Sugar Cookies
Pan de los Muertos
Pumpkin Muffins
Quick Strawberry Jam
Rhubarb Jam
Coconut Rice Pudding

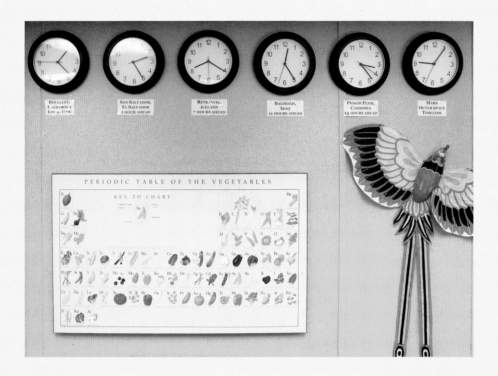

The piano in the kitchen allows for some spontaneous music to inspire the end-of-class cleanup, or a moment of daydreaming. A symbol in seeds of balance, harmony, nature, beauty, equilibrium.

David P.

I have learned that vegetables are better than I thought.

Aaron   Ms. Osborne
                                         5-6

I learned how fun washing dishes can be.

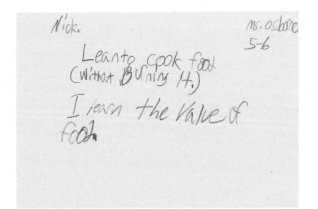

Nick   Ms. Osborne
                                         5-6

Lean to cook food (without Buning it)
I learn the Value of food.

Some interesting answers to the question of, "What have you learned in the kitchen?"

clarence

I learned
to cook

Markelly

I learned how to manage my
eating habits. I learned that how to
cut with out cutting my self

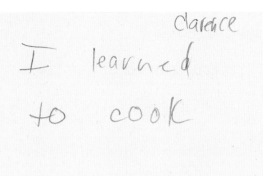

Zubeen

ms. Osborne
5-6° period

Something I learned in the
Kitchen is patience can
lead to being full.

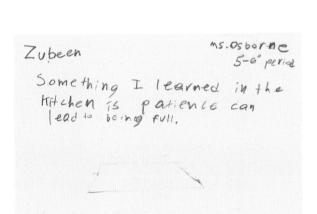

Students made individual tiles of their own design to beautify a wall that frames a raised bed in the garden.

(Pages 18–19) A bulldozer begins the process of removing the old asphalt, and breaks ground for the new garden.

(Page 44) A free-ranging Edible Schoolyard hen surveys her early autumn domain. Every day the students gather the eggs and hunt for snails to feed to the chickens, which helps keep the garden free of insect pests.

(Pages 46–47) The garden is a place to explore and follow the cycle of seasons. Foraging for ripe raspberries in the berry patch in late spring is a competitive sport.

(Pages 48–49) The hens are practically pets; they indulge students in their favorite game of seize-and-release tag played every day when school lets out.

(Pages 52–53) Math in the garden! Besides providing an ingredient for soups and pies, the winter squash harvest offers an opportunity for a hands-on lesson in circumference, measurement, weight, medium, and mean.

(Page 54) Gallons, quarts, pints, cups— students double-check their measurements while straining stock.

(Page 55) An eighth-grade student seasons a curry with fresh herbs from the garden, calling upon his senses, experience and skill.

(Page 57) Sixth-grade students write a personal "food memory" as part of their introduction to the kitchen classroom. Through this simple exercise, each child achieves success and a connection to the kitchen.

(Pages 58–59) At the heart of the school, the kitchen radiates simple beauty. The children know that all of the equipment has its place in the orderly kitchen classroom.

(Page 60) Cleanup after cooking and eating is a group activity. Spraying dishes and loading the dishwasher alongside classmates is real and pleasurable work.

(Page 60) The kitchen cooking classes conclude with a shared meal. Students and teachers sit down to enjoy the food they have grown, harvested and prepared together. Teachers prompt lively table conversation by introducing challenging questions for discussion.

(Page 61) Each kitchen lesson begins with an introduction to the recipe and a review of ingredients students have planted, tended, and harvested in the garden.

(Page 61) After school, the kitchen is a popular meeting place where friends can find a quiet place to collaborate on a homework assignment.

(Pages 62–63) Setting the table, with nice dishes and flowers from the garden, is part of creating an aesthetic, respectful place to gather to share more than food. Students learn table manners, the pleasure of serving others, and the calming effects of slowing down to listen and enjoy each other at the table.

(Page 65) Wild fennel, *Foeniculum vulgare,* is a primary insectary plant and an abundant source of the licorice-flavored seeds students use to flavor preparations in the kitchen. The tall feathery stalks are a native habitat for large green and black caterpillars that metamorphose into spectacular butterflies.

(Page 65) The kitchen altar connects students to time and place as they share events that affect their lives through drawing, writing and the placement of found objects.

(Page 65) Eighth-grade students introduce the Prince of Wales to the Edible Schoolyard kitchen classroom.

(Page 66) This Polish hen from our flock of different breeds is prized for her fabulous hairdo, her liking for being held, and her rose-colored eggs.

(Page 67) Esther Cook presents the recipe for the day and explains procedures and measurements. As part of a math lesson, the students are asked to double the ingredient amounts.

(Page 70) Turning the steaming compost pile is strenuous and fun. This compost took months of hard work to turn piles of garden and kitchen waste into a nourishing soil amendment. Along the way, students layered ingredients, recorded temperatures, and studied insect life in the steep mounds.

(Page 70) The Prince of Wales and students test the temperature of the active compost pile and discuss the ingredients and conditions needed to make nutrient-rich, organic compost.

(Page 70) Harvesting food and cooking it directly is an eye-opening and taste-expanding experience. Students are surprised to find vegetables they thought they didn't like to be delicious because of the "live" quality of ingredients that are freshly picked, when flavor and nutrients are their peak.

(Page 74) When the weather is fine, the feast moves outdoors. Some meals have a cultural or ethnic theme, such as soba noodles with various sauces and pickled vegetables. Students of different backgrounds can introduce their flavors of home to classmates.

(Page 75) Salads of all kinds and combinations are a mainstay of the kitchen classroom meals—tender lettuces, radishes, carrots, beans, tomatoes, cucumbers, edible flowers, and fresh eggs from the hens. Add some garlic croutons, arrange on beautiful platter, and call your friends to the table.

Acknowledgments

So many generous and hardworking people, over so many years, together created the Edible Schoolyard, and with it the dream of Edible Education. They include parents whose children are now all grown up, teachers who've moved on to other schools and even other careers, and volunteers from near and far. In the list that follows, I've done my best to name each and every one. But to those I've forgotten—and there are doubtless many—please know that the omission is purely accidental, and that you have my enduring gratitude.

Colin Anderson, former Assistant Teacher, Edible Schoolyard; Susan Andrews, former Executive Director, Edible Schoolyard; Zenobia Barlow, Executive Director, Center for Ecoliteracy; Tom Bates, Mayor, City of Berkeley; Adriana Betti, former 7th grade Math Teacher; James Bond, Sculptor and Story Teller; Barbara Boxer, U.S. Senator, California; Dave Brandon, Dave Brandon Signs; Janet Brown, Partner, Center for Ecoliteracy; Susie Buell, Philanthropist; Peter Buckley, Partner, Center for Ecoliteracy; Rebecca Burke, 6th grade Math & Science Teacher, King Middle School; Café Fanny; Dr. Fritjov Capra, Partner, Center for Ecoliteracy; Bob Carrau, Artist & Writer; Center for Ecoliteracy, Partner; Chelsea Chapman, former Program Coordinator, Edible Schoolyard; Chez Panisse Restaurant; Jay Cohen, 8th grade Science Teacher, King Middle School; Esther Cook, Chef Teacher, Edible Schoolyard; Kyle Cornforth, Program Associate, Edible Schoolyard; Scott Constable, Designer & Artist; Patty Curtan, Artist & Designer; Topher Delaney, Landscape Architect; Pamela Doolan, BUSD School Board; Terry Doran, BUSD School Board; Paul Doty, Berkeley Horticultural Nursery; Delaine Eastin, former State Superintendent of Public Instruction; Benjamin Eichorn, Apprentice Garden Teacher; Victoria Edwards, 7th & 8th Grade Humanities Teacher, King Middle School; Carolyn Federman, Development Director, Chez Panisse Foundation; Nancy Feinstein, Organizational Consultant; Fessenden Firewood; Molly Fraker, former Executive Director, Chez Panisse Foundation; Bill Fujimoto, Monterey Market; Josie Gerst, former 7th grade Humanities Teacher, King Middle School; Doug Gosling, Occidental Arts & Ecology Center; Green Gulch Farm; Marsha Guerrero, Director Special Projects, Chez Panisse Foundation; Akemi Hamai, 7th & 8th grade Science Teacher, King Middle School; Loni Hancock, Member US Assembly; Hands on Bay Area;

Karen Hansen, former 6th grade Math & Science Teacher, King Middle School; Lizbeth Hasse, Legal Counsel; David Hawkins, former Garden Teacher, Edible Schoolyard; Rebecca Hayden, Architect, Vilar and Associates; Bethanie Hines, AmeriCorps Member; Mildred Howard, former Executive Director, Edible Schoolyard; Shirley Issel, BUSD School Board; Wendy Johnson, San Francisco Zen Center, Green Gulch Farm Consultant to Edible Schoolyard; Lew Jones, Director of Facilities, BUSD; Juan's Place; Susie Kossa-Rienzi, 6th grade Humanities Teacher, King Middle School; Sibella Kraus, SAGE; Michele Lawrence, former School Superintendent, BUSD; Barbara Lee, U.S. Congresswoman, California; Genevieve Leslie, former 6th grade Humanities Teacher, King Middle School; Peter Levitt, Saul's Delicatessen; Linda Maio, Berkeley City Council member; Karl Linn, Founder, Peralta & Northside Community Art Gardens; Kermit Lynch, Kermit Lynch Wine Merchant; Occidental Arts & Ecology Center; Jim Maser, Picante Cocina Mexicana; Yvette McCullough, former 7th & 8th grade Science Teacher, King Middle School; Jack McLaughlin, former School Superintendent, BUSD; Lorinda Miller; Nico Monday, wood-oven builder; Susan Moore, Accountant; Joan Nathan, Curator, Smithsonian Folklife Festival, 2005; Joy Osborne, 6th grade Humanities Teacher, King Middle School; Ene Ostertas Constable, former Executive Director, Edible Schoolyard; Kit Pappenheimer, former Principal, King Middle School; Scott Parker; Patty Rathwell, 7th & 8th ELL Teacher, King Middle School; Buddy Rhodes Artisan Concrete; Amanda Rieux, former Assistant Garden Teacher, Edible Schoolyard; Nancy Riddle, BUSD School Board; Joaquin Rivera, BUSD School Board; Peter Rudnick, Farmer; Stanley Shadowed, Architect; Cristina Salas-Poras, Collaborator; Julie Searle, 7th grade English Teacher, King Middle School; Erik Seniska, Artist; Kelsey Siegel, former Garden Teacher & Manager, Edible Schoolyard; John Selawsky, BUSD School Board; Nancy Skinner, BUSD School Board; Neil Smith, former Principal, King Middle School; Catherine Sneed, Founder, Horticultural Program at San Francisco County Jail; Beth Sonnenberg, 6th grade Math & Science Teacher, King Middle School; Fritz Streiff, Writer; Leslie Stenger, former 6th grade Math & Science Teacher, King Middle School; Steve Sullivan, Acme Bread; Phoebe Tanner, 6th grade Math & Science Teacher, King Middle School; Nicole Thomas, Assistant Chef Teacher; Stephen Thomas, Artist & Director, The Oxbow School; Kathy Tierney, Landscape Architect; Alta Tingle, The Gardener; Beebo Turman, Founder, Edible Schoolyard Garden Committee & Documentarian; Tyler, Artist & Photographer; Jose Vilar, Architect, Vilar & Associates; Susie Walsh-Daloz, Garden Manager and Teacher; Eric Weaver, Attorney; Greg Williams, Custodian, King Middle School; Wendy Williams, Philanthropist; Carina Wong, Executive Director, Chez Panisse Foundation; Victor Yool, Berkeley Horticultural Nursery; all the students of Martin Luther King Jr. Middle School.

Alice Waters was born on April 28, 1944, in Chatham, New Jersey. She graduated from the University of California at Berkeley in 1967 with a degree in French Cultural Studies before training at the International Montessori School in London. Her daughter, Fanny, was born in 1983.

Chez Panisse Restaurant opened in 1971, serving a single fixed-price menu that changes daily. The set menu format remains at the heart of Alice's philosophy of serving the most delicious organic products, only when they are in season. Over the course of three decades, Chez Panisse has developed a network of local farmers and ranchers whose dedication to sustainable agriculture assures Chez Panisse a steady supply of pure and fresh ingredients.

In 1996, in celebration of the restaurant's twenty-fifth anniversary, Alice created the Chez Panisse Foundation. The Edible Schoolyard at Martin Luther King Jr. Middle School in Berkeley is the Foundation's primary beneficiary. More information is available on the Foundation's Web site, www.chezpanissefoundation.org.